The Violence

ahsahta press

The New Series

number 11

The Violence

Ethan Paquin

Boise State University • Boise • Idaho • 2005

Ahsahta Press, Boise State University
Boise, Idaho 83725
http://ahsahtapress.boisestate.edu

Printed in the United States of America
Cover design by Quemadura
Book design by Janet Holmes
Author photograph © Matt Lavatelli 2005
First printing 2005
ISBN 0-916272-85-0

Library of Congress Cataloging-in-Publication Data

Paquin, Ethan.
The violence / Ethan Paquin.
p. cm. -- (The new series ; no. 11)
Includes bibliographical references.
ISBN 0-916272-85-0 (pbk. : alk. paper)
I. Title. II. New series (Ahsahta Press) ; no. 11.

PS3566.A6235V56 2005
811'.6--DC22

2005011474

ACKNOWLEDGMENTS

The author gratefully acknowledges the editors of the following publications in which some of these poems first appeared, occasionally in different form: *Artvoice*: "Exit"; *Ecopoetics*: "Deep Wild"; *Fence*: "Range Peaks"; *Forklift, Ohio*: "Post-Post-Poem," "Rumination of Sad Object in Defiance of Metaphor," "Santa Lucia," "Shit Rust"; *Gulf Coast*: "Rustic I," "The Silence, the Rain and the Road"; *Parakeet*: "[people are/wherever there's clouds/starry curvature]"; *Pleiades*: "Why Do You Stand In the Window Nightly"; *Salt Hill*: "Corpse Over Ohio," "Divorce of Narcissus," "Sorrow"; *Sentence*: "Poetry is No Cure"; *Shade*: "Rustic II"; *Verse*: "Metametahead," "New Form"; and online in *Cordite:* "Muse Has Lost Her Lustre"; *Elves*: "After Christmas Poem"; *McSweeney's*: "Oratio Moderna"

Many thanks to those who provided inspiration, aided in this book's creation, and read various incarnations of it to offer advice: Dean Young, Sally Keith, Andy Morgan, Thomas Heise, Matt Hart, Martin Corless-Smith, Joshua Beckman, Daniel Nester, Brian Henry, Theodore Pelton, Christina Mengert, Dan Beachy-Quick, Peter Johnson, Graham Foust and Forrest Gander. My gratitude to Robert Creeley (1926–2005)—ever Onward.

CONTENTS

The Violence

[people are/wherever there's clouds/starry curvature]

people are killed out here, wherever there's clouds like
this
 you hear it in the rain you   glean it in the glare the dust
what whisper whimper hasn't of it ever been   said   and
say i know who the child is! who dreamt of the widest sky
ever   starry curvature   royal blue and being marooned
crushed neath it nearly and there came the animal in the
dream   there they ran   over dune one   dune two grass o
shake he's behind it. and now it's all done   for child is
a malleable meat

±

The second I thought it, wrote it, the world's tallest dam collapsed. Would
I suffer blame? And if not, why not? I am meant to   We all
relate, connect   We have all have we not sat darkened rooms, drapery
burgunded rooms, burnished rooms   mulch'd with our sin   burden
of some her on our mind   once   stood tallest on our world. What of the
others,   what's wrought over on them, those. They have high walls to
conceal their tall works. They have eight million river clocks.   Someone
please to tell time for the beneath, some agency.

pretty sunset bridge in
a dead-song

and you want the bridge to come alive
but it won't

and you want the word to come alive
and it won't

and you want the wife to come alive
and it won't

~

The *look* of punishment's   what we're
after here.

If you've seen the death crossing
a friend's face, you'll know I've not
seen a death.   I've witnessed an array.

CORPSE OVER OHIO

I don't like expressing myself in front of
funeral parlours.   I don't like grey flowers.

I feel the sting of the papercut every place
the clematis blossoms every noontime.

So you say you like weddings?
I do, too, but not their aftermaths.

Why must the sun shine in order for success
to enter the casket, chapel, garden, equation?

Enter the casket, chapel, garden, equation—
I feel the sting of the papercut every place.

I don't like expressing myself in front of
the clematis blossoms every noontime.

I don't like grey flowers.
I do, too, but not their aftermaths.

So you say you like weddings?
Funeral parlours.

A bird has his bones, if he rummages
deep spruce and hears them return
his cackling—something twisted about

the woods, how there's too much heat,
what that does exactly to energy. Sound,
movement, like that of ferns—catalogued

energy for the next traveler to borrow.
I can see generations of wings beating
and so can the friends who kill Girl A,

stoning her beside a mossy tributary
in which generations of blue-eyed lights
are convened and prettied. Before she dies

she utters the way you'll utter before
you die, before the birds ever heard
her utter. And the trees mightn't care.

DETRITUS

(#) = single space denotes a holding over of last hard consonant sound from the end of the previous line, or a drawing out of the last vowel sound from the end of the previous line.

(##) – double space indicates the sound of inhaling must be emphasized between end of previous line and start of new line : reaffirm life of the poem, life of the silence, life of the recital.

(*) – inflect "—" as a question.

I never wanted someone to die before— (*)   I never tried to imagine a gutted ___________
(#)
        I never thought to clean a sink—   riddled with womblike
  emphatic silence   and my blood!   —

It is fun, that blood,

it is fun, —

it runs like no other   I walked along a street called <u>Franklin Street</u> the other day

(##)

and the sky was like melting away. Sky misted into brick buildings. They:

stocky brick buildings and people live in them and that means they await:

in them. OK.

And now the walk reminds me of a sink because are the colours of porcelain

everywhere, why, Yes!   and God is so evil that he puts it everywhere and   all

of a sudden a sink is misted with some   blood like a building   that has got mist

made of clouds   all over   and he wants a few of us to suffer   so he makes me

think of blood all   the time   I walk   and gut this lamb,

gut it in to the sink,   Ha!, the photograph

of someone   who   might have been   my widow,

sprayed   with a lamb's flank   bloody'd

and no there   is no   christ imagery at work   here but

rather i merely wanted to eat a lamb for

i was hungry.   i walked because i was—   walking

to the store to—   buy a lamb and i was—   walking

in a bad neighborhood of year like a bad hue

of dead tree

DIVORCE OF NARCISSUS

And so what if she was in bed with that guy,
cut like from some burlap cloth on a steamer
bound for Galapagos—far-flung, grimy. My
stance hasn't changed since I was a senior:

I know love when I feel it and that's nightly—
flip on the t.v., put the pot to boil, dunk the bag
and spoon the sugar, forget about her—subtly,
whoever that her may be. I've always gone stag.

Why change. So what about her tortured interior?
I won't ever return. *Make your errors, darling, try
to endure.* In my dictionary you won't find "dirge";
in my eyes: . . . part apparition, fruit-bearer, deity,

well-wisher, assassin, rumbler, spiter, gourmand,
sender now of poesies tatter'd and mangled.

EXIT

washed summer with a wickedness
did i or was that god. . .   lake . . .

the wash looked pearl-like but was
not tiny fractals and parts.

til know nothing bestil me o lord
with true arboretae in such mists.

watching the lake i bothered
to know its agitation, not

to know the lake. looking at a pistil
is over there, not of some new mind

but a patient mind, barrel of dusts
kicked up. make your exit wind make

your break. flowers off at the stems
not scientific language or action

but the shearing is what concerns me
lake when i stare out at you god you

can have all my clouds. i have a shore
she sailed from and i waved goodbye

when from all the mists nothing came
from out of them.

MUSE HAS LOST HER LUSTRE

She'll still sleep with me, so that's not it—
the tin-like bark of that nameless tree did it. It was more
spectacular than her face, than swirling ribbons in a gaggle
of daughters, than the face of a possible affair-girl
which floated off into death-state
gently   as when rocks are born

Ablution when stitched with pertussisine hate.
Prosperity when evenly cross-hatched, suspicious.
Abortion when the begonia's is wax for a change.
Temerity when leaving through patches of birches.

Literacy when little grey movies in raindrops.
Convolution when pushing motion's empty square.
Piracy when sufficiently pent-up, photos/pixels.
Conflation when more is more is more, per se.

Easiest when all that's left is fruit or gamma's hiss.
Home-like when wallpaper pineapple patterned in prose.
Earliest when worms scurry, if they do, to the bushes.
Lake-like the air when she smiles, and for once I see.

*

She charred him.
Simple as that
telephone. No,
a crescent. Make
that a crescent,
maker. Poem
maker, thou
seated god—

the breeze is
windy today
like the hated

*

Like the hated revolving door
of its throat I make little sense.

I make little masks and think
about them they're great, even

good. So I give them to her
over and over, at night or at

never—some are not enough
nor good enough. They're off

cast. Like the eye cuts the moon-
chaff, all its extra lights, and gets

right down to the heart of it: moon
for what it is, Moon, ne'er shine.

*

If odes still existed I would write a sprawling one for [she].
If tomatoes still existed I would give just a dime more for love.
If beaches still existed I would run to a bodega for various sodae.
If people still existed I would get all the miniature accolades.
If modillions still existed I would paint all lawns with glee.
If Texas still existed, I would want to live in New Hampshire.

*

If [she] existed,
the [she] not
the [she]-chaff,

if my eyes could cut through the odes
and messages and breezes,
really hear or read or feel these
things, then I might be little. Happier.

Today my apple rolled away.

It is always a sad day when the skyline
looks bitten-off like a lost apple!

Yet it peers at me always, from down
the avenue and through all the trees.

I might be a little happier if there were none
and just this beach of the wandering mind.

I let her touch me in a way I will not let God touch me. God
will occasionally wake to wrestle with. I spit on his fires I
will not let them transport me. I will overlook the fire,
pain on my little toe. My left foot hurts, foot of the devil. My
hurt a pet apen to nurture. My pet tells me nature to discard.
If I discard the jewels I found I will not make it to heaven.
If I keep the hurt I can trawl it, yo-yo it, dawdle it, dangle it,
make it mine and your own. Make it mine again in a way it
was before it lacked its suffer. It was an empty little animal
trolling a yard made my own by my mere presence. I will
bottle my presence; they will have to buy it. They can not stand
to live the way other bottles tell them. They make so many
demands. They are pages to flip and ideas to catch and think
everything or nothing of. When they put their ears to the bottle
bottle hole as it were
they hear oceans of suffering. We will not stand for suffering. We
will stand for something other than the vast silence. But God will lose
if he spins a fire for I am more wretched than fire. Water is more wretched
than fire; so, fire is killed by water. Silences are filled with pets strutting
in the yard. I have made the continents my yard. I have to admit the feat
was unthinkable. I was spurred by some aching brightness. It was the colour
of coral's forehead. It was the colour of cliffs and her beach house stood
out would not stand without the emptiness of the ocean. Me it
writes, I write

ORATIO MODERNA

o the times you poured a dour muscatel,
god, bastard—you are the wrong god seated
for this, our new wilderness. there is trash
that appears friendlier than thou. some neon
accusations—"Hoagys" and "Live Strippers"
and "Oil-in-a-Minute"—what is this skyline,

what is the. here in this miniature skyline
there are shades of smoky musk. do tell
all the minions of the flesh—strippers,
pornographers, painters—to be seated
and await the sermon; they will as neon
tubes be jolted to awakening: no more trashy

thoughts. yes, you, my dear god, trash-
remover in the sky, lord of sky and circle and line
and my best teacher, beam revelatory neon-
bright awareness. all theology is so much musculature,
flex'd on the weak or wicked, supposedly. sit,
will you? listen—like water—that which strips

away the ___________ to a bareness. strippers
got it right: remove the rhinestones, that trash
(makeup, bras, ad inf.). they favour johns seated
in the front row in hats resembling the skyline

of Buffalo. they are, yes, intoxicated all by muscatel
and various human whiffs. look at all the neon

reminding us of how real it is, that goddamned neon—
ungodly invention, luring us in. all the strippers
got us hooked on their new breast versions. muscatel
never tasted so good, realer than psalmery. trashed,
one can saunter through a really tiny kitten's skyline
when hammered—gin, varied theocracies, etc. seated

at the podium, one can say "bitch-ass trick"; seated
at the podium, one can boom a voice distinct as neon
and farther and wider than any damned skyline
known to nobody but those 'in touch'—strippers,
minions of "hellish agency," professors, Eurotrash,
all knowledgable on their coke and shiny muscatel;

seated neath a neon skyline, bleach'ed strippers
and sluts and hardy priests, all cheap, all get trashed
on cheap and heady and varied, all heady, muscatels.

POST-POST POEM

"Cicero"
becomes
"Keats"
becomes
"Stevens"
becomes
"Ashbery"
becomes
"Bernstein"
becomes
"Paquin" :
and the critics
are right, my
poems are not
poems but they
are evidence in
a really dinky
box in a murky
corner of the
chain of human
stuff that will
soon be burned
like shit by sun
when trumpets
sound and poets,

whose work meant,
will be lifted and
saved while i will
pay for abusing
the only thing i
ever knew how
to use except my
penis and burn

PUNISHMENT

You'll find sometime where rain rains daggers in
down to persuade you. Like the matter discharg-
éd all about me as I smash a lamp with your gold-
en name amuletted in halo above   the light shine
below   my bleeding hand which would murder me
again and again and cast the body into a super-
fluous sea full of tyrants with horns and wings but
God thou tract of evacuated skyline I want to pry a-
part, and piss on, and pummel my face.

Landscapes, Part II.

Come on in, baselisk!

Come on in, cathedral!

I won't harm you!

I will only harm the small boy in La Gare,
who was by several creditors named Ivor.

I will only harm sixteen trees of the special variety
as defined by my expert sociology of soils.

I will only harm a sound balloon.

I will only harm the act of hovering.

See it alter!

I have altered it already, while you wasted time
in a green box over there in a ticket-price dust.

I will only harm the range peaks which conspire
as ever to make sure flies keep breeding and coming.

What a place that is untouched by a fly—I will drink
happily there, or, I would also splice my life-halves there.

I will always think of a quiet nomad!

Are you that nomad? nomadine?

All this while desert browns a bit more.

All this while because how can it stop.

Desert because there are the copses.

Trip on them!   Can you?

How many blasts did I just hear?

A blast can hover.

This haunt.

I hate it here. I am damned by the quiet charge to
live in the thrust balance between weight and height,

between black and white as in one of the paintings.

After I have left her insides I start to go colourless.

I wish I knew if I was

           . I think I might. Some women have seen it
in my eyes supposedly. I want to believe

in red, in the women. In the sky's faith.

Come on out, sky!

Come on, beach!

There are so many trawlers . . . green, indigo.

Come on in, boats!

You've been admirably beaten . . .
don't take any more.

Will you?

Yes, we learn from the boats, which stay

out tossing all night and every night.

Which have been cut away?

Out each morning they go.

Out and out. Tears on the face of the sea,
asterisks on the breath of the landscape.

All the faces moving away.

All the harm done moving away.

Here is my handful of flies and some summits
in a paper sack. These will stay.

Will the boats come in?

All the faces moving in.

All the harm done moving in.

To remind me to stay moving, give me this shawl.

RUMINATION OF SAD OBJECT IN DEFIANCE OF METAPHOR

There are many beautiful women to sleep with,
many beautiful women I want to sleep with

and I'm become a hatchet that looks toward
doing the event and being placed atop a stump

by the anxious hand that conducted the event
~~with it~~ with me just moments before. Then the red

and I glanced over at ______________ e'er calm
because of this: I was the barrister of unique energy.

. . . Through use I'm made more sore than a vagina so
I might complain, but don't. Beautiful women there are

I want to sleep with, . . . beautiful branches glimmering, . . .
dying leaves peering down on my own little object-ness.

on deciding against some word :

one page's worth of thought to come
toward   not to that decision

(the scythe coming toward not to

wheat   of which we've all partaken
golden and   when hacked

                    the scythe has come to stalk

and shattered : air in its approach,
stamen and stalk in its arrival

RUSTIC II

her word is falling
from the roadside

the weak would ask *Why is it that you fall from me*

but I am not weak   just
overcome by heights

new evidence puts me high up
in some territory, some yellow

territory, not exactly dusty,
not exactly what I'd hoped

her hair would do to the sun,
filtering cliffs with its wavure

cliffs in her hair / from or of her hair

SANTA LUCIA

*

William wants a boat and that is all he wants.
A charter boat, modest, not a sloop, streamlined.
Guests pepper him for drinks and that is all they want.
I sit with William who is too nervous to smoke.
He wonders about vagaries, securing a bank loan.
'Why is it impossible for me to do what I want'—
I paraphrase our three-hour-long conversation
because one wants not wallow in powerlessness.
A good American I am, editing all the ugliness
and hopelessness. My, the Santa Lucia sunset tonight.

*

I bought shells from a beach vendor. Conch,
two small glassy ones and a larger, pink, peeling
one with a hole carved in the end to trumpet out—
to charter boats, tourist divers, potential marks.
Vendors, the way they saunter on volcanic sand . . .
the way they slice across Anse Cochon, *Bay of Pigs,*
Americans lounging all about, avoiding the sellers
in their sea kayaks coming south from Canaries,
town straddling the line between shithole and kingdom—
brightest place ever, vibrant paints and plants. Smiles,
requisite laundry creek, herkyjerk drivers. "Emerald sea."
Never one thought of language or composition
though so much sand, stones. Moving tiny words
around like so many precious stones I am
in order to relay the utter lack of order in an indecent
noon day sun content to wither me as a shell.

*

Yes the numerous beers and drinks and octopus dishes
at the fish festival—Anse la Raye, Friday night, back
in Buffalo it's the fish fry but here, *lambi* and 'pot fish'—
'that's what they call the unknown fish they catch,'
throw it all in a pot, everything from the net, let it boil.
Buses from the resorts clamber in all night. Tourists mill.
Seedier nightclubs than in Brooklyn. (You New Yorkers,
so full of yourselves. Anyone in New York City ever say
'men's bathroom . . . right over there' and point to a beach?
In your tough fantasies, maybe . . .) Michael Jackson imitator,
his friend 'filming' the dance with a fake camcorder. Chaos?
Wonder of the universal energies. Piton lager beer, bottle
by bottle by bottle. Lexus Liberalism, baby—'well, at least
we're here, buying the fish they caught, not off at the resort
eating a fancy dinner.' Piton by Piton by Piton. Happy energy.
Woozy street dances between young newlyweds. Two white faces
in a sea of black faces. Invaders, perhaps. It is scary to see
the minimum amount of tolerance in the eyes of so many.

SHIT RUST

Shit, rust,
you found me now.

I'm in need of a multiphonic outrider.

I want to go atop a demilune.

Do you worry when you're oxidizing and I'm merely scribbling?

Or, so that children will understand,
do you worry when you commit
me to murder me?

I like being palatalized by rain!

I always have trouble in town.

You help me hide from all the towns,

*

The rain is free to make mistakes.

Don't ever doubt when you see it twirl
it's in error.

To make mistakes
the rain must be free.

To rain mistakes I will
but not on you.

Every night I will the rain off
and this is why it rains harder.

You must know my leaf,
it is a powerless one.

Maybe you'll have some bright ones
for me to borrow— for me, so dun,

to take. The sun must care for you—

*

I like . . .   —you're real like a leaf
which blows about a bit.

The leaves blowing about lend colour
to this world.   Yet one leaf

stands out with no use for the others;
stand out with no use for the others'

but only for mine   eyes.

am going
going electric in

[constant violence of man
toward animal]

meander

*

a* green tree
is like a* green tree,
is like a* green tree's
materiality.

[* hold *a* as in an
incantation]

little cups of fire all around.

*

how'd i come to think of
                                        the cliff—
how'd i come to the cliff—
let me cough   it's cold as all
                    burn'd boughs—
cinders to float from the brink
                    to the river
like a riddle—how   air
                    do you dwindle—
fires like to eat you   grey
                    ballast—

*

two sloops,
eight-hundred sloops,
seventy-thousand-odd whitecaps,
nine-hundred-thousand-odd swells,
twenty-six-million salts resolves
to blast my little shore.

littlest cove

little Pomona

hang thy wreath round my neck
on this heated sand.

point to your hidden air.

billions of warmnesses. and
men on the boats are after them.

THE SILENCE, THE RAIN AND THE ROAD

Who'd have guessed we'd traverse a territory so cleared
of hard pain, yet full of the storm of beauty, the pain ~~of dust~~
of knowing it's never the same dust, of knowing the yellow
heights of cliffs at five p.m. will differ always, mutability, change,
fixity, [perennial obsessions], but in Vale or in Idaho City or in
Anse Cochon or in Ripton or in Buffalo always the dust, a yellow,
the worry of who the companion must be until the companion's
face is reflected in a half-developed sunrise, river's run, fiery july,
when it all becomes obvious, or as obvious as it will ever be. Rain
plies onward in restless sleep, re-gathering over the lakes and all,
and so do we. And so it goes with all these gone places, now silences
made salient by hard roads not so interested in us at all, now silences
made awful by rains not so interested in the hope of sunny metal objects,
warm days, cloud-reddened harbours—we've got to find some noise out there,
silence is too pale:
. But the wind is pleasant to walk in!,
and so I walk in it. It's easy to ignore the sunset when wrapped
in a breeze because I traverse wind all the time and have no piano
common to the sun, which is vicious. I know how harsh white kitchens
appear in five a.m. sunrise, so I stay out of the kitchens except when
to kill an ant or two. I know the dust, I know the yellow, and if you
know mc you will know that rain and dust and yellow appear in so
many of my forests. I know how to enter the wind. Who'd have guessed
this? I bruise myself there, the silence.

THE VIOLENCE

I bestow upon thee, with this ochre, the violence.

A swatch for you and I.

We can recline and take note of the leaves' thigmotaxis—

this summer God hates us
and's put it in the wind.

Colours so very so very bright
                    and bright today and good
  for all our moods, all our sour stomachs.

It's a humid hour, jussively aggressive

sickening & he's captured it well—
cutin greens and custards, navies,

forget about God

Little leaf little leaf little leaf.

I think the second one spied the third
and then, me.

Now at an easel
there's littler recourse
than to paint
and drink

in the neighborhood

's arboreal dystrophy

and converse with friends
I never will
be because I am
not quite me—or
God—

lost halfway between

+

fearing not the lonely try
saith hill and arroyo,
spring, entablatures pebbledashed
orange, late afternoon *try*
fearing not the lonely

objects in space o byways
objects in space o shadow
forms, skirtings and noonal slides,
krummholz and kurdt dry
fearing not the lonely *try*

to scrape it out here try

+

March 2004
[sun
+
time]

one year ago, roadsiding on Owyhee Canyon

—a year later, listening to Medardo Rosso
through his sculpture speak disfigurement

—disfigurines

—Medardo Rosso at Owyhee planning
his melted faces

Futurist cliffs for they scream an American
patriotism of solitude in minor oranges

Rosso's sui generis cliffs for they chute
in blight, grasp for a pass/ed God,

He of Beautie and Renewalle—
white as sperm, that hope . . .

+

des fugues

you are

+

carside, fundamentalist radio

carview, hurt-orange white
chickens

Today in 2086, the year I will die,
things will be much worse—

the wrong Gods seated,
minor plagues in blue or . . .

like, a violet not quite invented,
not quite ready deveil\ed so

through an infernal __________________ and sea
where were you

through rainless orange seasonal
where were you

through burn cycles and fealty
where were you

through plant and reap and germinal
where were you

through scree in mountainside fall
where were you

through mixed or extended metaphor
where were you

through threshers and silos and sów

where were you

through man and the death of violence toward beast
where were you

where were you
though man and his beast and his violence did die?

where were you
though threshers and silos and sów pitch-perfect in sun?

where were you
though metaphor wither'd for your stare categorizable's not?

where were you
though scree whispered to the mountainsides, "Fall"?

where were you
though planted were things of regrettable harvest?

where were you
though burn cycles took out the canopy in which [your eyes]?

where were you
though rain-drownings quelléd orange burn of sun and nightly?

where were you
though an __________________ sea toss'd you, stopped you,

whereas my harbour you'd have sought,

whereas my hand to drowning sun offered,

whereas my water to singe the sides of leaves,

whereas my scythe and seeds and immutable hunger,

whereas my pulley to raise any and all of the peaks as a god,

whereas my stare to meet yours, for if not mine, then whom,

whereas my brush to auric light digest and mirror your eyes,

whereas my gravestone to the violence of language,
insufficient and stupid in the line of a gaze

so heavily levied,

and readily,

and in levity,

in levity am I constant   and   in energy   yours
—touch   where were you   touch   this
life can not   stand   length

of shadow   of shadow and nightly
and nightly your   shadow   stand   close
in   please   where   to see.   to
see no   more shadow   but
the woman   she stands   essence
but   always dissolvéd   some-
how.   and come   closer   sea,   sea-
scape's   all   we have   got,   reminder
of hunger   auric light   eat
sun offered   shadow a   form   of
sun,   she a form   of   frozen light,   dis-
solvéd   little   leaf in   field
of vision   field   of   leaves   each a
future   each a   harbour   as
are those   her   eyes

VIGNETTES

upon the New Year, 2004

days of 200-pound hundred-year-old windows crasht on the hand,
universes of falling not stoppable by a net,
cascades of torrents of streams and rivulets are jealous,
dyings and dyings wrought over in new blood metalature,
asides and backtalke pours your new friend the neighbour,
silvery light!,

**

when we walked the Kinsman Ridge that was about six years ago,
and now your alternator or whatsooth is broken or somesuch,
and now the snow, height of steam, falles on us in Buffalo, N.Y.,
weight of how many hundreds of miles away the peaks are.

what difference? Like, that your hair is now falling and your skin peeling
in the tub more than ever before? Or, say you preferred not a skinless
existence,
one bereft of follicle and pellicle, leaving your innards for all to see,
can't you at least admire the brown mung at the little mouths of the drain?

what difference that you used to love me and now have a kind of tempered
love for me?

are the mountains too boring to themselves?

**

cache of light cache of plaster
cache of cactus cache of counter
cache of cashew cache of gift
cache of videodrome of signage
cache of carafe cache of xenia
cache of pretty windows' chance of sky

Whan that Avril with its showres kicks your ass with cold,
remember how much worse it is in February and even
(syn. = level) your head. Be calm, stay that way.
It's easy with Zoloft, easier with your Dreamcatcher.®
Live the double-spaced life, leave room for captions,
imagine what Andy Capp would say about your folly,
like when you threw the fridge out for fun and, lo,
a U.S. Olympic Team discus captain happened to drive
right past you and see the toss, and he said, "Hey!
I see talent in you! Join us!" and you begged him off
because you had no more room for organizations.
"Piss off," you said, "I have no room for organizations
in my life." And that was it. Imagine the caption. It's
April and you're thinking of that, as well as February,
as well as how to stay calm, as well as how to heed
my prescriptive advice. There's a lot to digest here.
Stare at the fucking freezing rain, is all you wanted
in the first place and all I find beauty in anyway—
not the rain but in the staring, the head's white place.

There are things to be said in a poem and things to not be said and some of the latter things include: a recipe for pilaf! How metrical that would be! This is a zanier wordlife I've got now that my wife took me back now that I think god is a mannequin

POETRY IS NO CURE

Lowneath those thar hills are issues not yet identified by famed psychiatrists, and all around. How does it feel to live in a sick world? *Aw, Christ,* the neighbors will say as we finish up the unpacking process, *not another bunch of cynics. Ma, do we really need them damn cynics movin' in next dur?* Lots of sentences in our neighborhood have been left incompleted. For it to be any other way would depend on a quick solution, the like of which poetry does not promise. Something that can be written about is the lack of promises in poetry, the lack of promising poetry. It flutters uselessly about all the alleys, but the drunkards are sure to leap every once in a while to try and land one. Land one and frame it on the big bay window wall in the foyer. *Aw, shucks, ain't that pretty. Like Greece.* Fluttering arbour/hills

ALL THINGS OVERWHELMED

I once had a thyme sprig! What did I do with it? There were a few things I *wanted* to do with it. I *wanted* to make it accumulate some wealth, but it wanted to be a wreath. I thought it looked good in dirt but it hated purple. (Yes, dirt can be purple. Ever been to Rumney?) It wouldn't, so, try anything on. I would lecture it every evening! They were excellent evenings, full of chartreuse and andouille! But, one eve, then the sky turned like Boise or something and all the kids wanted to do was want it. A lot of hands reached up to grab it all but you can't grab the sky, not even little portions of it, so there was a bunch of wasted time that evening and subsequent evenings. Wasted time all accumulated. Like snow in Idaho City, but not in Boise, which is in Idaho and not too far off from the I.C. (as the kids call it) but is much warmer and in a sort of valley. All the hands thrust up in the sky every night in this tiny valley, but the most beautiful thing was that fucking thyme sprig. It fit as I wish I on a shoe lace.

AFTER CHRISTMAS POEM

Look!   Bubbles do not appear as they once were!

*

If I dream of frost, do you truly mean I will be as wet as the dream?

*

A certain winter light, not that other winter light?

*

Leaf encased in ice, ice in love and obviously!

*

Skies can prescribe their icy shoals, let them go ahead. I sit now, won't set out until I feel like slipping.

*

Thank you for this tea, love, and did you know anything about this?
How there is but one day, which happens to be today, when we can return to stone one another.

WHY DO YOU STAND IN THE WINDOW NIGHTLY

*

Why do you stand in the window nightly

awaiting my return
or some other watch

A trickle will not wash away the boulder

awaiting you in the rivulet
in the high high mountains

Why do you pace and veer toward the trees

slumbrous cold in the groves
October grove or August grove

A trickle will not wash away the boulder

*

Where are the words you broke
with a thimble,

and where are the pins you made
into clear homes for thunder

and vegetable—ply a root, will you
please, and show some tendance.

In my lack I will find a water
fit for the listener; will you

listen: you are a branch afloat
but close friend to the sky at one

and demon at two and rapids
at all other hours of the rainlight.

*

Old words come like prophecies,
epitaphs for failures then unseen
and now realer than seed blight.

The garden has a patch and another
and one tree is green to the fullest
but for a plane of decay I project.

The shutters are metal and bent
at the corners whereyond I always
wanted to peer. Who, what now.

And what do you want to become
of me? A point on the line of elms,
drooping, sentries of the long street?

A stone to scold or stroke or supply
with friendly stones in the garden?
A beached mastiff post-rescue?

There is little left in the largesse
of a universe like this one, all drawn
for the dusk and ready to turn in.

*

Who, what now. There is little left
hand turn, little right hand turn.
Then beyond, a loud sight of dusk.

And beyond, a space the weight
of square and blue, where words
we can read from outside the window

and bestow on ourselves the slip
of going light, going grasses, and from
the going, naught that is graver than gone.

NOTES

"Corpse Over Ohio" was written in an airplane with Kelley Paquin.

"Owyhee" is for Joshua Beckman.

"Peel'ed Moon" borrows "revolving door / of its throat" from Christina Mengert.

"Sorrow" is for Samuel and Elise Paquin.

"Sparism" is for Sally Keith.

"The Violence" is for Dean Young.

What eventually became the book's title was Andy Morgan's idea. Many thanks to him for giving me his blessing to use it.

ABOUT THE AUTHOR

ETHAN PAQUIN is the author of *Accumulus*, released by Salt in 2003. He created and has been editor of the international poetry journal *Slope* (www.slope.org) since 1999, and in 2001 founded the small press Slope Editions. His poetry has been published throughout the U.S., Europe and Australia, and his criticism appears in journals including *The Boston Review, Verse* and *Canadian Review of Books*. A native of New Hampshire, he directs the Creative Writing Program at Medaille College in Buffalo, New York.

Ahsahta Press

Sawtooth Poetry Prize Series

2002: Aaron McCollough, *Welkin* (Brenda Hillman, judge)
2003: Graham Foust, *Leave the Room to Itself* (Joe Wenderoth, judge)
2004: Noah Eli Gordon, *The Area of Sound Called the Subtone* (Claudia Rankine, judge)

New Series

Dan Beachy-Quick, *Spell*
Brigitte Byrd, *Fence Above the Sea*
Lisa Fishman, *Dear, Read*
Peggy Hamilton, *Forbidden City*
Charles O. Hartman, *Island*
Sandra Miller, *Oriflamme*
Ethan Paquin, *The Violence*
Lance Phillips, *Corpus Socius*
Lance Phillips, *Cur aliquid vidi*
Heather Sellers, *Drinking Girls and Their Dresses*
Liz Waldner, *Saving the Appearances*

Modern and Contemporary Poetry of the American West

Sandra Alcosser, *A Fish to Feed All Hunger*
David Axelrod, *Jerusalem of Grass*
David Baker, *Laws of the Land*
Dick Barnes, *Few and Far Between*
Conger Beasley, Jr., *Over DeSoto's Bones*
Linda Bierds, *Flights of the Harvest-Mare*

RICHARD BLESSING, *Winter Constellations*
BOYER, BURMASTER, AND TRUSKY, EDS., *The Ahsahta Anthology*
PEGGY POND CHURCH, *New and Selected Poems*
KATHARINE COLES, *The One Right Touch*
WYN COOPER, *The Country of Here Below*
CRAIG COTTER, *Chopstix Numbers*
JUDSON CREWS, *The Clock of Moss*
H.L. DAVIS, *Selected Poems*
SUSAN STRAYER DEAL, *The Dark is a Door*
SUSAN STRAYER DEAL, *No Moving Parts*
LINDA DYER, *Fictional Teeth*
GRETEL EHRLICH, *To Touch the Water*
GARY ESAREY, *How Crows Talk and Willows Walk*
JULIE FAY, *Portraits of Women*
THOMAS HORNSBY FERRIL, *Anvil of Roses*
THOMAS HORNSBY FERRIL, *Westering*
HILDEGARDE FLANNER, *The Hearkening Eye*
CHARLEY JOHN GREASYBEAR, *Songs*
CORRINNE HALES, *Underground*
HAZEL HALL, *Selected Poems*
NAN HANNON, *Sky River*
GWENDOLEN HASTE, *Selected Poems*
KEVIN HEARLE, *Each Thing We Know Is Changed Because We Know It And Other Poems*
SONYA HESS, *Kingdom of Lost Waters*
CYNTHIA HOGUE, *The Woman in Red*
ROBERT KRIEGER, *Headlands, Rising*
ELIO EMILIANO LIGI, *Disturbances*
HANIEL LONG, *My Seasons*
KEN MCCULLOUGH, *Sycamore•Oriole*
NORMAN MCLEOD, *Selected Poems*
BARBARA MEYN, *The Abalone Heart*
DAVID MUTSCHLECNER, *Esse*
DIXIE PARTRIDGE, *Deer in the Haystacks*
GERRYE PAYNE, *The Year-God*

GEORGE PERREAULT, *Curved Like an Eye*

HOWARD W. ROBERTSON, *to the fierce guard in the Assyrian Saloon*

LEO ROMERO, *Agua Negra*

LEO ROMERO, *Going Home Away Indian*

MIRIAM SAGAN, *The Widow's Coat*

PHILIP ST. CLAIR, *At the Tent of Heaven*

PHILIP ST. CLAIR, *Little-Dog-of-Iron*

DONALD SCHENKER, *Up Here*

GARY SHORT, *Theory of Twilight*

D.J. SMITH, *Prayers for the Dead Ventriloquist*

RICHARD SPEAKES, *Hannah's Travel*

GENEVIEVE TAGGARD, *To the Natural World*

TOM TRUSKY, ED., *Women Poets of the West*

MARNIE WALSH, *A Taste of the Knife*

BILL WITHERUP, *Men at Work*

CAROLYNE WRIGHT, *Stealing the Children*

This book is set in Apollo type with ITC Oficina Sans titles
by Ahsahta Press at Boise State University
and manufactured on acid-free paper
by Boise State University Printing and Graphics, Boise, Idaho.
Cover design by Quemadura.

AHSAHTA PRESS
2005